W9-BPL-949

A Storybook of Saints

ELIZABETH HANNA PHAM

A
STORYBOOK
of
SAINTS

ILLUSTRATIONS BY CECILIA VU

SOPHIA INSTITUTE PRESS
Manchester, New Hampshire

Copyright © 2020 by Elizabeth Hanna Pham

Illustrations Copyright © 2020 by Sophia Institute Press

Printed in the United States of America. All rights reserved.

Cover design by LUCAS Art & Design, Jenison, MI.

On the cover: Floral border (1073972327) © John Erickson / Shutterstock.com.

Interior design by Perceptions Design Studio.

No part of this book may be reproduced, stored in a retrieval system, or transmitted in any form, or by any means, electronic, mechanical, photocopying, or otherwise, without the prior written permission of the publisher, except by a reviewer, who may quote brief passages in a review.

Sophia Institute Press
Box 5284, Manchester, NH 03108
1-800-888-9344

www.SophiaInstitute.com

Sophia Institute Press® is a registered trademark of Sophia Institute.

Library of Congress cataloging-in-publication data has been applied for.

ISBN 978-1-64413-068-1

First printing

To Saint Nicholas, who started it all

CONTENTS

Note from the Author

The saints in this book are all different from each other. Some lived a long, long time ago. Some lived only a few years ago! Some we know very little about, and some we know a whole lot about.

In this book, I've told many "historically accurate" stories, especially about the more modern saints. But I've also included many legends.

When a story is a "legend," it doesn't mean that it isn't true. It simply means that we don't know for sure that things happened in that exact way. But even if things didn't happen in that exact way, we know that the legends are born out of something that *did* happen.

George may not have slain a real-life dragon, but he did fight the dragon of paganism and he did fight the devil. We just don't know exactly what that devil looked like.

The important thing is that all the saints in this book are real people who lived holy lives and who pray for us from

Heaven. One day we'll know the rest of their stories—the rest of the pieces of the puzzles.

And they'll be even better than the precious fragments that we have here.

A STORYBOOK OF SAINTS

NICHOLAS

Feast Day: December 6

It was going to be a sad winter.

My mother and father barely had enough money to buy our daily bread. Certainly, there would be no grand or merry midwinter's feast.

Worse, these were the last few weeks I was to spend with my mother and father and little sisters. To feed the rest of the family, my father planned to send me far away to work. It would not be easy work. I would be lonely and would miss my sweet, warm home and my loving family.

Then, one evening as I lay awake, praying that I might be rescued from my terrible fate, I heard a faint sound coming through the howling wind. *Footsteps.* They were heavy—a man's footsteps.

I was afraid. Did he mean us harm?

I lay still and listened.

Suddenly, I heard the footsteps stop. Then, a rustling sound, a gruff voice, and something jingling—almost like bells! I sat up in bed, opened the window wide, and looked out.

Just as I did, a tiny red bag soared right past me and landed in front of the fire.

The footsteps rushed away as I peered into the darkness to see who it was.

I was too late.

So I sat down by the fire and opened the little bag.

Inside were more gold coins than I'd ever seen in my life! I jumped up with joy and ran to wake my family.

My parents used those gold coins to feed our family and, years later, to pay for my wedding.

In fact, I was married by the man who was my secret gift-giver, Bishop Nicholas, the most beloved man in all the land. It turned out to be such a happy winter!

It's now been many years since Bishop Nicholas saved my family. He went on to bring faith, hope, and love to hundreds of other people . . . and he still does today.

But I will always be the first little girl to have received a gift from Santa Claus.

SAINT NICHOLAS

Born in Modern-Day Turkey, A.D. 270
Died in A.D. 343

Saint Nicholas was the bishop of Myra. He was well known for his generosity to the poor, children, and those in difficult situations. He is beloved all over the world and often goes by other names, such as Santa Claus and Father Christmas.

Juan Diego

Feast Day: December 9

When that man first came to me and told me that the Virgin Mary had appeared to him—appeared to him and told him to ask me to build a church!—I didn't believe him.

Mary doesn't talk to just anybody, I thought. *Especially not here.*

Besides, as bishop in this pagan town that had only just heard about Jesus, I already had enough to worry about. What I really cared about was peace for my people. I wanted them to be able to worship freely and safely. I didn't have time or money enough to build a new church just because someone claimed that Mary wanted one.

How was I to know that she had really appeared to him? How was I to know that she really wanted a new church? I couldn't.

So I sent the man away and thought he wouldn't come back.

But Juan Diego did come back and told me again about Mary's wishes.

So I said, *Bring me a sign. Prove to me that Mary really said all this.*

He left, and I was sure this time I would not see him again.

But, again, he returned. This time he said that Our Lady had given him the sign I requested. *She told me,* Juan Diego said, *to gather roses from the hill where we met and bring them to you.*

That caught my attention because it was December, a time when roses don't generally bloom here in Mexico. *Show me the roses,* I said.

When Juan Diego opened his cloak, dozens of bright roses tumbled out.

But that's not the most remarkable thing. Almost covering the inside of the cloak was a bright picture of Mary, a perfect picture, one nobody could have painted or drawn. A picture that surprised me and would soon surprise the world.

So I had my people build a chapel here on Tepeyac Hill. In it we hung the picture of Mary that had appeared miraculously on Juan Diego's cloak.

Over the centuries since then, tens of thousands of people from all across the world have come to see that picture here in what was once just the little town of Guadalupe — the little town that hardly knew Jesus.

Mary brought us Jesus. And the whole world came with her.

Saint Juan Diego

*Born in Mexico, 1474
Died in 1548*

Saint Juan Diego is well known for his pious and obedient heart and his visits with Mary. To prove to the bishop her desire that a church be built there, Mary performed a miracle that made her beautiful picture appear on Juan's tilma. The precious tilma now hangs in a church in Mexico, and thousands of people come to venerate it every year.

LUCY

Feast Day: December 13

Lucy lived in a dark, dark world. The Roman emperor hated Christians and wanted to destroy them all. But Lucy was not afraid of the darkness. She was too filled up with light!

Lucy carried her light wherever she went. And people noticed her. It wasn't long before the Roman emperor noticed her too. He heard about her faith. He heard how she had given her heart to Jesus. He heard how she planned to give all her money to the poor.

And he hated her for all of this.

He hated Lucy's light, so he decided to put it out.

He sent his soldiers to seize her. They tried to drag her from her home, but she was too strong, so they tied her to a team of oxen. The oxen pulled her into the street.

The soldiers stacked piles of wood around her and laid burning torches on the wood. They were determined to put out Lucy's light. They would put out her light with fire.

But fire can't put out fire! No matter how hard the soldiers tried, the wood around Lucy wouldn't burn and the fire never touched her.

Eventually, the soldiers got frustrated by Lucy and her strength and the strength of her God who could work such amazing miracles.

So they decided to kill her quickly, with a sword.

Lucy finally died.

But before she died, she told the Romans that, soon, their evil empire would come to an end. Christians would be free to worship their God. The light would shine in the darkness, and the darkness would not overcome it.

Lucy was right in her predictions.

Just a few years after her martyrdom, the Great Persecution ended.

Lucy became a great saint, beloved by all the people, bringing light to them and to many more generations of God's people across the world and throughout the centuries.

SAINT LUCY

Born in Italy, A.D. 283
Died in A.D. 304

There are many stories about Saint Lucy's strong faith and heroic bravery in the face of horrible violence. It is even said that the Roman soldiers took out her eyes! This, along with the meaning of her name and the fact that her feast falls near the shortest day of the year, has led many Christians to celebrate her joyously as a symbol of light.

John the Evangelist

Feast Day: December 27

John loved Jesus. He followed Jesus wherever He went and never left His side. John was there when Jesus preached on the hillside. He was there when Jesus called the little children and held them and blessed them.

John was there when Jesus healed and saved. John was there in the boat with Jesus, and John was there on the seashore. John saw Jesus's tears, and he saw Jesus's laughter.

John was there when Jesus broke the Bread of Angels and held it up for the very first time. When Jesus foretold that He would be taken away from the disciples, John was right beside Him.

And that grieved John sorely. *How can this be?* he asked himself. John had finally found the one his soul loved, and he could not let Him go!

15

Then came that wretched Friday, the day the Savior of the World let angry soldiers nail Him to the Cross. The other Apostles were so afraid, so horrified, that they ran away.

But John stayed. He clung to Jesus's every last word. John was not going to let Him go.

Jesus had not told John the whole story yet. Not about the glorious Sunday to come or about the forty days of Easter rejoicing. Or about the tongues of fire that would come to fill them up with the grace they needed to withstand time's short separation. Or about the Heavenly Kingdom and its endless treasures. That would happen later.

For the moment, Jesus merely looked down upon John and loved him. He saw John's tears and his trembling, his aching heart. *Please don't go,* it cried out silently.

Jesus knew He couldn't stay, but He wanted to give beloved John a part of Himself.

Looking first to His mother, Mary, and then to John, Jesus said to John, *Behold your mother!*

After Jesus died, John took Mary into his home. John took care of her, and she took care of him. Their hearts ached, and they often cried. But in Mary's eyes John saw Jesus's eyes. In Mary's smile, he saw Jesus's smile. And in Mary, John found again the One his soul loved.

And John didn't have to let Him go.

SAINT JOHN THE EVANGELIST

*Born in Israel, circa A.D. 15
Died circa A.D. 100*

Saint John was very close to Jesus—he is often referred to as the "disciple whom Jesus loved." He sat next to Jesus at the Last Supper and stood next to the Cross on Good Friday. John wrote one of the Gospels, three epistles, and the book of Revelation. He is the only Apostle who did not die a martyr and is said to have miraculously escaped many attempts on his life.

THE HOLY INNOCENTS

Feast Day: December 28

Many years ago, there lived a greedy and selfish king named Herod. He loved nothing more than being king.

So when Herod heard that a new king was coming, he grew angry.

When he found out the new king was a little baby, he grew even angrier.

This shall not be! thought Herod. *Only I am king.*

So he gave his soldiers a terrible command, the worst command he'd ever given. The worst command anyone could ever give.

Go! he told his soldiers. *Go and kill all the babies! That way, none of them can be king.*

Herod's soldiers obeyed that terrible command.

Warned of Herod's plans by the angel Gabriel, Joseph, Mary, and little Baby Jesus fled into Egypt, so the soldiers never found the new King they were looking for.

But they found many other baby boys. And it was a dreadful, horrible night.

Years later, on a dark and dreary Friday, the Roman soldiers killed Jesus, the same King that Herod had sought so many years before.

This time, the King was all grown up, and He had a plan.

The next day, right after He died on the Cross, Jesus went down into the place where all the saints before Him were waiting. There He found Moses and Miriam, Noah and Joseph, and a host of other good men and women. He carried them all up to Heaven, where there was great rejoicing!

But the greatest rejoicing of all was for the children ... for the little babies who had so long ago been victims of the violence of Herod.

King Herod may have loved his bejeweled crown, but his crown is dust now.

The most beautiful crowns rest on the heads of those children in Heaven, where they reign like kings and queens above.

While the world grows old and grey, they stay always young and pure.

Heaven has always been a merry place, but it is even merrier now because of those children.

We call them the Holy Innocents.

THE HOLY INNOCENTS

Born in Israel, First Century A.D.
Died in the First Century A.D.

The Holy Innocents were the many babies slaughtered by King Herod in his effort to find and kill the Baby Jesus. We do not know their names. We do not know exactly how many of these babies there were. But we know that they are precious to Jesus. And in their littleness and meekness, they are holy and powerful.

MARY

Feast Day: January 1

It was a warm, spring morning when I first saw her, the woman of grace, walking into the temple with her husband and her young son.

From far away, she looked like any other woman, but when she turned to face me, her eyes were all love and peace. Her son had the same look in His eyes. They were the happiest family I had ever seen.

No wonder I was surprised, some weeks later, when I heard that the boy, Jesus, had gone missing! Mary and Joseph searched Jerusalem for two long days but there was no sign of Him. Surely, such a good boy would not run away or hide or do anything to worry His parents. Had He been kidnapped?

Finally, on the third day, Mary found Him.

And He was right where she'd left Him! Right there in the middle of the temple. He was talking with the priests.

When young Jesus saw His mother, He said to her, *Did you not know I would be in my Father's house?*

We all heard Him say it, and we braced ourselves for her response. What would she do to Him? Would she yell and scold Him? Surely, she was dreadfully angry. Surely, she would punish Him and never set Him free in Jerusalem again.

But when I looked at the face of that woman of grace, I saw no anger at all. Mary didn't yell at her little boy. She didn't threaten or punish Him. She didn't ask lots of questions. She didn't say anything at all!

She just wrapped her arms around her dear son and held Him close. Even though she didn't understand.

Twenty years later, on a warm, spring morning in the streets of Jerusalem, I saw that woman of grace again.

This time, too, she was looking for her Son.

She found Him ... on the top of a hill, nailed to a cross.

When they took His body down, she didn't yell at the Roman soldiers. She didn't threaten or punish them. She didn't ask lots of questions. She didn't say anything at all!

She just wrapped her arms around her dear Son and held Him close. Even though she didn't understand.

Mary, the Mother of God

*Born in Israel, First Century B.C.
Assumed into Heaven,
First Century A.D.*

Mary was a simple girl, born to simple parents in the town of Nazareth. When the angel Gabriel appeared to her and told her that she would be the Mother of God, she obediently accepted the task, caring for and following Jesus throughout the many joyful and painful steps of His life. She reigns in Heaven now as our Queen and Mother and loves us with a tender, perfect love.

Caspar, Melchior, and Balthasar

Feast Day: January 6

It was the best feast we'd ever had—the night we dined in King Herod's palace. There were dates and figs and soft, creamy cheeses, and the finest cuts of meat. There were dancers and musicians performing for our delight. We were wise men with treasures of our own, but never had we seen anything like Herod's palace!

And he promised us that we could partake of it whenever we wanted, as long as we would show him the way to the prophesied King of the Jews whom we were seeking.

And why wouldn't we show him?

Later, all the way through those winding little streets we spoke of the great fortunes Herod might give us. Maybe he would make us his own trusted advisers! That shining star in the sky held so much promise.

But when we finally arrived at the place where the star shone the brightest, all our plans stopped short. Beneath it was only a little house, sleeping quietly. Too little for a king. Certainly, too little for a king.

But prophets don't lie.

So we walked up to the little house, timidly, quietly, so as not to disturb the strange calm we felt there.

A young woman came out. Was she a servant?

She smiled gently and lifted up the bundle in her arms. Suddenly, from it shone forth light brighter than the star that shone down upon it. And the most wonderful thing in the world lay in the bundle: more beautiful than the gold we carried, more sacred than the frankincense, and more sweet-smelling than the myrrh.

Then the Babe smiled at us!

We fell upon our knees.

Shortly after we left that precious Holy Family, an angel came in the night and told us not to return to Herod.

But we already knew that.

So we set off for our separate homes.

We knew that when Herod found out, he would be angry.

We weren't sure what he would do to us, but we didn't care anymore. Not about palaces or treasure. Not about soldiers coming after us. We didn't care anymore.

Because we'd just seen the Kingdom of Heaven ... and nothing on earth was better than that.

CASPAR, MELCHIOR, AND BALTHASAR

Birthplaces Unknown
Born in the First Century B.C.
Died in the First Century A.D.

The Magi were wise men who studied the stars and the Scriptures—both of which led them to the prophesied King, the Baby Jesus. They gave Him gifts of gold, frankincense, and myrrh, and they did not return to Herod, fearing he might harm Jesus. Some say they were martyred for this act of disobedience. But their faith and wonder live on and inspire the nations.

THOMAS AQUINAS

Feast Day: January 28
(traditional: March 7)

Thomas didn't really like to talk.

Of course, he had plenty of things to say. He had plenty of thoughts running around in his mind. But his words never seemed to come out right.

Sometimes he preferred just to think his thoughts rather than try to explain them to people who might not understand … because people never seemed to understand.

The other boys in school called him a "dumb ox." A dumb ox!

Thomas *was* a big boy and he didn't say much, so they must have thought his head was full of straw!

Then one day, seated at his desk in the classroom, Thomas finally spoke.

What is God? he asked.

And nobody knew the answer.

Even though they all went to Mass and said their prayers, nobody could answer Thomas's question.

So he decided to ask God to help him answer it.

God did help him. In fact, God filled Thomas's mind with wisdom.

After that, Thomas asked more and more questions—so many questions that he had to write them down, and his writings filled dozens of books.

People started reading those books. All sorts of people! Kings, princes, smart people, wealthy people, poor people, young and old people, priests, doctors, teachers, saints and sinners, believers and unbelievers.

Thomas's books helped people understand who God is and why and how we should follow Him. They helped people understand everything. The dumb ox wasn't so dumb after all.

Hundreds of years later, people are still reading the books he wrote!

Shortly before Thomas's death, Jesus appeared to him and showed him many wonderful things about Heaven. These visions filled Thomas with joy and peace, but they also made him feel small—as if he had nothing left to do or say.

Thomas told his friends that, compared with the wonders of Heaven, the many beautiful words he had written were just like straw.

But there is nothing wrong with straw.

God once slept in straw, right next to an ox.

Saint Thomas Aquinas

Born in Italy, 1225
Died in 1274

Saint Thomas Aquinas was a quiet but brilliant and holy young man. When he was nineteen, he left home to join the Dominicans and became a priest. Thomas went on to write the *Summa Theologica*, a large book on philosophy and theology that has educated and inspired truth seekers for centuries.

BLAISE

Feast Day: February 3

I wanted to do something to help the good doctor.

After all, he was always helping everyone else.

He had healed men and women and children. He had healed dogs and cats and bears and birds.

One day, he even rescued my little pig from the horrible clutches of an angry, hungry wolf! He simply ordered the wolf to drop the pig, and the wolf obeyed. Maybe he obeyed because the good doctor had once healed him too!

But then they took the good doctor. They found him in his cave in the wilderness amongst the animals, and they arrested him and put him in prison! Blaise was a good doctor, but he was a good bishop and a good Christian too. And the pagan government did not like that.

We all knew what they would do to him.

But I wanted to do something to help the good doctor.

35

I knew I could not set him free. The wolves had cornered Blaise, surrounded him. And I knew I could not rescue him as he had rescued my little pig. I could not save him. I could not heal him.

But maybe I could make him feel a little better.

So, in a flurry, I gathered up all the candles in the house. And I ran to the prison. Through the bars I handed the candles to Blaise. *To read your scripture by . . . and to give you light,* I told him. The good doctor smiled. And then I realized he didn't need me to rescue him. He wasn't afraid at all.

The evil governor killed the good doctor and bishop, Blaise. But nearly two thousand years later, on February 3, the priests in church bless the throats of the faithful with two candles tied together. Candles like the ones I gave to Blaise. And the good doctor still helps those who seek his intercession. The good doctor still heals.

SAINT BLAISE

Died in Armenia in 316

Saint Blaise was a bishop and a physician of bodies and souls, of humans and animals. For a long time, he lived as a hermit in a cave, and it is said that wild beasts would often visit him. He was eventually captured by the government and taken to prison. On his way to prison, he miraculously healed a little boy who was choking on a fish bone; hence his association with ailments of the throat.

JACINTA

Feast Day: February 20

Little Jacinta loved to dance. When she danced, it felt as if the whole world danced with her. Her heart was full of happiness, and her happiness made other people happy too.

But then suddenly, Jacinta stopped dancing. She became more serious and distracted. She stopped paying attention to the music around her. It seemed as if she was listening to something else.

Jacinta *was* listening to something else.

For the past few months, Mother Mary had been visiting Jacinta and her brother and her cousin and speaking to them.

Mary said that she wanted to save the world and its people from the attacks of the devil, and that the children could help her do this. Mary knew that sometimes the very smallest people are also the wisest and the strongest.

But Mary told the children that if they were to help her, they would first have to see and learn things about the world that were painful to see and learn. Mary showed the children Hell—the place where people go when they do not want to be with God.

After Jacinta saw this—after she saw what sin does to people—she no longer felt that the whole world danced. She no longer felt like dancing herself.

But then one day, Mary told the children that she would show them—and the rest of the world—a miracle. Hearing about this promise, thousands of people came on the appointed day to watch as the children knelt in a field and waited for Mary to appear there.

It was a rainy day, dark and dreary. Suddenly, the sun broke through the clouds. The sun was brighter than ever, but somehow it didn't hurt their eyes. It flashed in many beautiful colors and then—best of all—it began to *dance*!

When she was only ten years old, Jacinta became sick and died.

On this earth, she never danced again. But she didn't mind. For Mary had promised to take her directly to Heaven and to take many other people there too—people Jacinta had helped to save.

Together now in Heaven, they all dance as the sun did that day, on and on, in beautiful light, for all eternity.

SAINT JACINTA MARTO

Born in Portugal in 1908
Died in 1919

Saint Jacinta and her brother Francisco and her cousin Lucia were visited by Mary multiple times at Fatima. During these visits, the children endured many sufferings but also learned profound secrets and witnessed many miracles. Jacinta died when she was only ten years old. She is the youngest saint to be canonized who was not a martyr.

PERPETUA

Feast Day: March 7
(traditional: March 6)

Perpetua always tried to make her soul beautiful. But she liked making her hair beautiful too! She had long, wavy hair, and she liked to braid it and curl it and tie it up with pretty little pins.

Even after carrying a baby in her belly for nine months and after giving birth to that baby and nursing him and rocking him when she was very, very tired, Perpetua still did her hair beautifully. As if she were on her way to meet a king!

One day, not long after the birth of her baby, Roman soldiers came to arrest Perpetua because they knew she was a good Christian and they hated Christians. The soldiers seized Perpetua and took her to a prison. The prison was only a waiting room. The soldiers planned to kill Perpetua, along with other Christians.

But they weren't just planning to kill them. They were planning to kill them in a most violent and ugly way. They were going to send them out into the arena to be devoured by wild beasts!

As horrific as her sentence was, Perpetua did not let fear consume her. Behind the walls of the prison, Perpetua held her baby close and prayed and sang and encouraged the other prisoners to keep their faith alive.

Soon it was time for Perpetua to meet her death.

They took her out into the middle of the arena, and then they let loose a wild boar. The boar charged at Perpetua and, with its tusk, tore straight through her leg. She fell to the ground. Surely, she would never rise again.

The crowds waited nervously for the wild boar to finish her off.

But then, in the midst of this utter horror, amidst the blood and the violence and the dirt and the evil, something beautiful happened.

Perpetua stood up, proudly smiled, and, taking one of her lovely pins, tied up her lovely hair.

For Saint Perpetua knew she was going to meet her King!

Saint Perpetua

*Born in Modern-Day Tunisia,
circa A.D. 182
Died in A.D. 203*

Perpetua was a pagan noble-woman who decided to become a Christian. Shortly after her conversion, she was captured, taken to prison, and eventually killed by wild animals. But during her imprisonment, she kept her faith alive and helped encourage the other prisoners. And she was well remembered for her fiery, bold courage in the face of a gruesome death.

PATRICK

Feast Day: March 17

Patrick was only sixteen when pirates kidnapped him from his happy home in Britain and took him as a slave to Ireland.

Ireland was a strange land. Its people believed strange things and worshipped strange gods. Many of the Irish people were not friendly to Christians, and Patrick often feared for his life. Without armor, shield, or sword, Patrick had no way to defend himself.

So, Patrick decided to pray. He prayed during the day and during the night. He prayed that Jesus would always be with him. He prayed that Jesus would be his shield and his armor:

Christ with me,
Christ before me,
Christ behind me,
Christ in me, he prayed.

As he prayed, Patrick's fears began to subside. Courage flooded his soul. He didn't know how long he would be stuck in Ireland, but he knew that Christ would be with him.

Seven years after his kidnapping, Patrick escaped back to his home. His family was overjoyed, and Patrick felt that all his prayers had been answered.

But not long afterward, God surprised Patrick with a message in a dream: *Go back to Ireland! Go back and teach the Irish people about Jesus!*

The last thing Patrick wanted to do was return to Ireland, but he trusted God, and so he went.

At first, the Irish were angry at Patrick's return, and even more so for his trying to spread the message of Jesus. They didn't want to give up their pagan ways. Twelve times they tried to kill Patrick, but he prayed even harder and his strong prayers continued to shield him:

> *Christ beneath me,*
> *Christ above me,*
> *Christ on my right,*
> *Christ on my left,*
> *Christ when I lie down,*
> *Christ when I sit down,*
> *Christ when I arise.*

Eventually, the people grew interested: *Patrick, who are you? What makes you so strong?*

And they let Patrick teach them about Jesus.

Soon, Patrick had baptized thousands of Irish people. Churches were built all over the country. Pagan Ireland put on the armor of Christ, and over the next thousand years, the Irish people carried the faith all around the world.

Today, many people still recite the prayer of Saint Patrick. It shields them and makes them strong.

It can make you strong too.

SAINT PATRICK

Born in Great Britain, A.D. 387
Died circa A.D. 493

Captured by pirates and brought to pagan Ireland, Patrick is credited with converting the Irish people to Christianity. He freed the beautiful green isle from many dangers and evils. Some even say that he drove out all the snakes! To this day, people of all nationalities love Patrick and celebrate his feast day with great enthusiasm.

JOSEPH

Feast Day: March 19

Joseph did not sleep enough.

He tried, but there was always too much to do.

Things to build. Things to fix. People to help.

And after Mary came along, dreams began disturbing Joseph's sleep. In one of those dreams, the angel Gabriel appeared to Joseph and told him he would be the father of the long-awaited Messiah!

This dream kept Joseph up, pacing back and forth.

He was just one man, a simple carpenter! How was he to guard and protect the most precious treasure in all the world?

Now he really had no time for sleep!

Then came that command from Caesar Augustus: *All men, return to the land of your birth.*

It would be a week-long journey from Nazareth to Bethlehem, and the Baby Jesus was about to be born! Joseph was worried they wouldn't make it in time. So he walked quickly.

Over rocky ground that battered his feet, through deserts that parched his throat, and through cities filled with fierce Roman soldiers. He walked until long after the sun had gone down.

And each night when Mary lay down to rest, Joseph stayed up, keeping watch so that nothing could come and harm her and the Baby.

Even the donkey rested more than Joseph.

When they finally got to Bethlehem, Joseph could barely keep his eyes from closing and his feet from stumbling, but he pressed on. They would soon reach the village's little inn. There, Joseph could finally rest!

But the inn had no room for them, and no one else in town would open their doors.

That night, Joseph could find shelter for his little family only in a smelly, dirty stable. There he gathered the cleanest, freshest straw for Mary to lie on and used the rest to fill the manger. None was left for Joseph. Again tonight, he would not sleep.

Death is often sad and painful, but not always; and it was not so for Joseph.

Many years after that night in Bethlehem, Joseph lay in a real bed. Mary, his lovely queen, held one of his hands, and Jesus, his precious little boy, held the other. Quietly, sweet Saint Joseph died, smiling.

And there he finally found rest – rest far better than sleep.

SAINT JOSEPH

Born in Israel, First Century B.C.
Died in the First Century A.D.

Saint Joseph was a hardworking carpenter, the loyal husband of Mary, and the gentle, kind foster father of Jesus. During his life on earth, he protected his little family and showered them with love. For two thousand years, people have had great devotion to Saint Joseph as the protector of families and fathers, the terror of demons, and, next to Mary, the greatest of all the saints.

BERNADETTE

Feast Day: April 16

Bernadette didn't like answering questions. She got so many of them in school. And she was often tired; her head hurt. Many times, she didn't know the answers at all.

Bernadette preferred to be at home, away from all the other children and all the questions. Family chores tired her body, but at least she could rest her mind and her heart.

One day, while Bernadette was busy with one of those family chores, a mysterious lady visited her. Appearing suddenly out of the mist on that cold February morning, the lady was dressed in blue and she was very beautiful. In fact, she was more beautiful than anyone Bernadette had ever seen.

She was radiant, shining, perfect. Her eyes contained within them all the happiness and sadness of the world combined. It made Bernadette wonder. It filled Bernadette with questions.

Who are you? Bernadette begged the lady.

But the lady would not answer Bernadette. She only smiled.

Days passed. Bernadette returned many times to the grotto where she met the mysterious lady. The lady told her many things but continued to refuse to answer Bernadette's question.

Meanwhile, everyone else was asking *Bernadette* questions.

They wondered if Bernadette was telling the truth about her visions. They wondered if she was crazy. They wondered, could they come and meet the lady too? They wondered about the miraculous water that came bubbling up where Bernadette dug in the mud at the lady's command.

Where did it come from? Was it holy?

Bernadette didn't know the answers. But she kept going back to the lady.

Because Bernadette's bishop also began demanding answers, the lady finally told Bernadette who she was.

Tell the Bishop that I am the Immaculate Conception, she said.

Bernadette didn't know what that meant, but she didn't need to know.

She already knew the lady by the light in her eyes and the warmth in her smile. She knew the lady was Mary, her own Blessed Mother.

About that, she didn't need to ask any questions.

SAINT BERNADETTE

Born in Lourdes, 1844
Died in 1879

Saint Bernadette was a weak, sickly child, but she was good and holy. At a grotto in Lourdes, Mary appeared to Bernadette many times, and a miraculous spring bubbled forth at the spot of Mary's appearance. Today, thousands of pilgrims travel to find healing at the grotto in Lourdes.

GEORGE

Feast Day: April 23

I was always a good soldier.

I was brave and I was strong.

I wasn't afraid of injury or even death!

And I always obeyed the commands of my emperor, Diocletian.

But then one day, Diocletian gave me a new command: *Go. Arrest all of the Christians!*

I couldn't do that. I, myself, was a Christian! And my fellow Christians had done nothing wrong.

Diocletian liked me. He liked that I was a good soldier. So he tried to convince me to listen to him and to go along with his wishes. He brought me to his palace and offered me all sorts of bribes. He offered me gold coins and fine robes and jewels. He offered me servants. He offered me a higher position in the army. He offered me whatever I might want.

All of this could be yours, he said. He even told me that I could still remain a Christian, in secret, as long as I followed his commands.

But I knew that wouldn't work.

If I followed Diocletian's commands — if I hurt the innocent — I would no longer be a Christian — I would no longer be a follower of Christ.

So I mustered my strength. Stomach churning, voice quivering, I faced Diocletian and told him the truth. I told him that I wanted to obey him. I wanted to be a good soldier. I respected him as my emperor, my king.

But I had another King too. A greater King. A stronger King. A better King. And that King's commands came first.

Diocletian flew into a fiery rage. Like a hungry dragon, he seethed and stomped and screamed. He ordered my immediate death, and told my executioners to be sure that my death was slow and painful and horrible.

I was afraid. I was afraid of that terrible dragon.

But I was still a good soldier.

A *knight*, the Christians would later call me, a *knight*.

I was brave and I was strong.

I obeyed the commands of my King, Jesus Christ.

And I went straight to Heaven.

SAINT GEORGE

Died in A.D. 303

Saint George was a Roman soldier but also a good and faithful Christian. He was eventually martyred for his Faith by the emperor Diocletian. There are many stories about George slaying dragons and protecting the innocent. We do not know whether these were real dragons or the even scarier evils of paganism. But we do know that George fought them bravely.

GIANNA

Feast Day: April 28

You don't have to do this, you know. We can do a surgery and make it all go away.

The doctors pleaded with Gianna. Gianna was a doctor too. So she already knew all about the sickness growing inside her womb.

But Gianna was also a mother. And she knew that the most wonderful thing in the world was also growing inside her womb.

A baby girl.

This baby girl was small and weak and quiet. Only her mother could feel the soft movements of her tiny arms and legs. Nobody knew what she was going to look like or what she was going to do in the world.

To the world, she didn't matter very much. That's why the doctors told Gianna they wanted to remove her womb, even though the baby girl lived inside it.

If we don't remove your womb, you will die from the sickness, they told Gianna.

But if they did remove her womb, the baby girl would die. What was Gianna to do?

Gianna prayed. And Gianna remembered Jesus. She remembered how Jesus told us not to be afraid of death. She remembered how Jesus told us that love is bigger than death. She wanted to give her baby life, even if it meant she might lose her own.

So Gianna told the doctors not to do the surgery to take out her womb.

Inside her mother, the little baby girl grew stronger and stronger every day. Gianna spent many wonderful days with her other children—teaching them, playing with them, cooking meals for them, singing with them, tucking them into bed at night, and praying with them. She knew that life on earth does not last forever, and so she spent those last days showing her children how much she loved them.

On Holy Saturday, the eve of the most wonderful day of the year, baby Gianna Emanuela was born. A week later, her mother, Gianna Molla, died.

Saint Gianna Molla's four children are still alive today. Although they miss their mother, they are happy because they know that when they were tiny, tiny babies, their mother's love gave them life, protected them, and helped them grow strong.

And it still does today.

SAINT GIANNA MOLLA

Born in Italy, 1922
Died in 1962

While pregnant with her fourth child, Gianna developed a dangerous complication. The doctors suggested a surgery to save her life, but it would destroy the life of her child, so Gianna refused. She joyfully chose her child's life over her own and died a week after her baby was born. But her sacrificial love flows down upon her children, and all of us, through her heavenly intercession.

JOAN

Feast Day: May 30

Your highness, there's a little peasant girl here to meet you. I assume you want me to send her away? The king never had time for such petty matters, and I was just trying to do my job.

But the king was in a casual mood that day, not dressed in his usual royal garb or seated on his throne, and I guess he was feeling a little playful.

Maybe he was intrigued by the peasant girl—I couldn't imagine why—but with a sly smile on his face he whispered to me, *Let her come forward. Just don't show her who I am. I'm going to stay in the crowd with all of you and see if she knows me.*

I chuckled to myself at the king's folly. *Knows you? She probably doesn't even know her own name!*

But when I turned back to the girl, I saw her already coming forward. Boldly but gracefully, she found her way straight through the crowd, right up to the king!

She bowed before him a perfect bow, as if she had been raised in this very castle and not in the poor outskirts of the country.

God give you life, gentle king, she said slowly and steadily in a voice strong and pure.

My eyes darted toward the king, wondering what he would do.

He stuttered, unsure, and then, his impish smile returning, he said, *I am not the king. He is!*

I stumbled backward as the king pointed at me.

One of his pranks, I guess. Maybe he was testing the girl to see what she would do. So I stood tall and raised my head, ready and willing to scold her as the pretend king.

But the girl did not get up from her bow. In fact, before I could say anything at all she spoke again, addressing the real king, *In God's name, gentle king, it is you, not him. I know it because I saw you in a dream.*

My mouth dropped open, but the king's smile widened.

What is your name, girl? the king asked, kindly.

I'm Joan.

Last name? he asked with eyebrows raised.

I don't know it, she said, brushing off his questioning. *But I know how to win the war.*

Saint Joan of Arc went on to help the king win the war, but we still don't really know her last name.

SAINT JOAN OF ARC

Born in France, 1412
Died in 1431

At an early age, Joan received visions of saints, who told her that she was supposed to lead the French army. It was difficult to convince other people of her mission, but they eventually listened to Joan, and she led them to victory. After the war, the English army captured Joan and killed her. But she died a brave martyr and a hero of France.

ANTHONY

Feast Day: June 13

Nobody wanted to go to Rimini. The town was full of sin and heresy. The last thing its people wanted was a visit from a Franciscan Friar.

So the friars mostly left Rimini alone.

But Anthony was different. He had a deep love for lost souls. He didn't give up on them easily. And he knew how to speak to them. His homilies were full of wisdom and truth. If anyone could change the hearts of Rimini's people, it was Anthony.

So he set off, filled with hope and confidence.

But when Anthony got to Rimini and started preaching, he found that no one would listen to him! In fact, the leaders of the town *ordered* the people not to listen to him.

Anthony didn't know what to do, but he wasn't going to give up. Especially not on lost souls.

He decided to go for a walk.

When Anthony came to a river at the edge of town, he looked down at the water and saw the fish swimming around in it. The sight of God's beautiful creatures doing exactly what He intended them to do filled Anthony with the same hope and confidence he'd felt on his way to Rimini.

Suddenly, Anthony stood tall, and, smiling, he spoke to the fish:

You, fish of the river and sea, listen to the Word of God, because the heretics refuse to hear it!

Immediately, hundreds of fish obeyed Anthony, swam toward him, and poked their little heads out.

Surprised but filled with joy, Anthony began his homily.

The fish continued to keep their heads out of the water, holding still and attentive, politely listening to everything Anthony had to say!

More fish came and then a few people, attracted by the spectacle! One by one, more and more people came to see the remarkable preacher to whom even the fish would listen.

At first, those people were just curious, pointing and whispering. Then, they began to listen. Finally, their hearts were moved.

That day, Anthony converted the whole town of Rimini, and the people gave up their sinful ways.

Anthony went on to preach and teach and save more lost souls.

And somewhere on the shores of lovely Italy, there swam some very special fish.

SAINT ANTHONY OF PADUA

Born in Portugal, 1195
Died in 1231

Saint Anthony was a Franciscan friar well known for his wisdom and beautiful homilies. He is often pictured with the Baby Jesus, and some people speculate that the Baby Jesus once visited him. Saint Anthony is beloved for his help in finding lost things, as he once patiently recovered his favorite and precious book along with the prodigal novice who had stolen it.

THOMAS MORE

Feast Day: June 22

It was a bright summer day, the worst day of my life. I walked through the streets of London in a daze. I walked to my father's execution.

My father had served King Henry; he had served King Henry well.

Then King Henry became greedy and selfish. He wanted to change the laws so he could cheat and steal and keep what didn't belong to him.

He wanted my father to help him do that. He wanted my father to lie.

But my father would not lie. Because of that, King Henry put him in jail.

To tell you the truth, I *wanted* my father to lie.

When he was in prison, I visited him and did everything I could to convince him to do what Henry wanted him to do.

Lying seemed like such a small thing, really. *Just tell a little lie, and the king will let you go!* I wished he would tell that lie, because then he wouldn't have to die.

I thought that if my father died I could never be happy again. Without him, the world would be dark and confusing.

But that morning, as I watched him climb up onto the scaffold, the world was bright and glorious. I didn't want to look. My heart swelled with pain and dread. But I had to look. And when I did, I saw a smile on my father's face.

No. That wasn't a smile. My father was *laughing*!

As he walked up those steps to his death, he told a joke! The crowds were amazed, as was his executioner, who, moments before he killed my father, begged my father for forgiveness. My father forgave him, and even gave the man a hug and a kiss.

What kind of faith was this, this faith of my father?

When that final moment came, I saw the sun shine down on his smile. I was glad he had not lied.

Soon after my father's death, miracles began happening because of him. People started calling him a saint: Saint Thomas More. I missed him terribly, but I knew that our separation was only temporary. And I felt his love surrounding and protecting me.

The day my father died *was* the worst day of my life, but it got better after that. His faith made me strong.

SAINT THOMAS MORE

Born in England in 1478
Died in 1535

Saint Thomas More was a devoted father and husband, a renowned lawyer, and a holy man. King Henry VIII took a liking to him and made him Lord Chancellor. But when Henry left his wife, married another woman, and declared himself head of the Church, Thomas More refused to support him. The king had Thomas More thrown into prison and executed.

JOHN THE BAPTIST

Feast Day: June 24

People thought John was crazy.

He almost never spoke. He slept in the wilderness like a wild man. He wore scratchy camel skins and ate nothing but honey and grasshoppers. Most people stayed far away from him.

But then one day, John came out of the wilderness. And he started talking.

He had a loud voice. A beautiful voice. And that loud voice said beautiful things.

People started to listen.

Then, they started to follow. They followed that voice back out into the wilderness. They sat on the dusty ground and listened closely as the voice echoed among the trees.

It told them that a Savior was coming—very soon!

God was coming down to earth to save them from their sins.

He is coming! the loud voice rang out, and the people listened.

One day, the voice led the people to the river. Then John, with his great, strong arms, plunged them, one by one, into the water. At first, the people were afraid, but the water felt clean and fresh, and the voice sang out words that changed them inside. They knew that what John said was true and good.

But then, suddenly, the voice stopped.

The whole world went silent.

A new man stepped into the water. He spoke to John quietly, and John spoke quietly back. John laid the man back and baptized Him, just as he had done the others.

Then the world began to shake! The clouds ran away from each other. The sky split right down the middle, and a piercing light burst through the crack as down through it swirled a white bird that gently settled on the shoulder of the newly baptized man in the water.

A new Voice shattered the silence: the loudest Voice — maybe even the loudest sound in the whole world, but it didn't hurt their ears. Everyone knew it was the voice of God, a voice like music, but it wasn't singing.

This is my beloved Son, it said.

Suddenly, John the Baptist didn't seem so crazy anymore.

Saint John the Baptist

*Born in Israel, First Century B.C.
Died circa A.D. 28–36*

John the Baptist was one of the first people to recognize the presence of Jesus when he leapt in the womb of his mother, Elizabeth, at the Visitation. As a grown man, John lived in the wild, eating locusts and honey and preaching the coming of the Savior. He was the first to perform baptisms, and he baptized Jesus Himself. John died a brave martyr at the hands of King Herod.

Simon Peter

Feast Day: June 29

Nervously, Simon Peter watched as Jesus moved among His friends with the water bowl and the towel.

Oh no, is He coming to me?

Simon Peter's feet were dirty. They smelled like mud and old fish. He had cracks in his heels and scabs on his toes. He had barely any toenails left. What would the King of the Universe think of those feet?

(*I made them*, He'd say.)

But Simon Peter wasn't sure.

Just as he wasn't sure in the boat when Jesus told them to drop the net into the water just one last time, and when they pulled it up, hundreds of fish tumbled out.

Just as he wasn't sure that time when Jesus, walking on the water, said to him, "*Walk! Walk to me!*" even though there was no dry land to walk on.

So, when Simon Peter stepped out of the boat, he soon sank down into the water because he didn't believe it was possible.

Not for human feet like his. About that, Simon Peter wasn't sure, so he sank.

Lord, are You going to wash my feet?

Jesus looked deeply into Simon Peter's eyes and loved him.

And then Simon Peter remembered. He remembered the marvelous, impossible things that happened when he trusted Jesus. He remembered what it felt like to walk on water.

Unless I wash you, you have no part with me.

So Simon Peter let Jesus wash his dirty feet.

Three days later, those dirty feet ran as fast as they could to see the impossible—a man risen from the dead! Then those same dirty feet traveled all over the world, telling people about the impossible. Telling people about the great and mighty King of the Universe. Telling people not to be afraid. Telling people that God loved them—even all the broken, dirty parts of them.

Then, one midsummer's day, soldiers who did not understand Jesus's message of love crucified Simon Peter, just as they had crucified his King. But because Simon Peter was not the King, he asked to be crucified upside down.

So Simon Peter's dirty, holy feet pointed up to the sky. But he was not afraid because he trusted that Jesus was in charge. Jesus was going to raise him up and give him a throne, and his dirty feet would walk in the Kingdom of Heaven.

SAINT PETER

*Born in Israel, First Century B.C.
Died in the First Century A.D.*

Simon Peter was a simple fisherman until Jesus called him to be one of the Twelve Apostles. Despite his weaknesses, Simon Peter was full of a deep and abiding faith. Jesus eventually made him the first pope. Simon Peter was martyred by crucifixion, but he requested that his cross be turned upside down, as he did not feel he deserved the same death as Christ.

MARIA GORETTI

Feast Day: July 6

Alessandro was a sinful young man. He didn't follow the commandments. He didn't care about other people.

Maria was a very good girl. She was kind and helpful and brave. Her soul was clean and white as snow.

Alessandro knew Maria was good, and that annoyed him. He tried to convince her to stop following the commandments. He tried to convince her that life would be more fun if she sinned.

But Maria remembered what her mother had told her, that it was *never, ever worth it to sin.*

One day, Alessandro became so annoyed with Maria's goodness, so angry at her for her refusal to sin with him, that he attacked her. He hurt her badly and then left her alone and ran away.

A Storybook of Saints

Maria's family found her and rushed her to the hospital. The doctors tried to do surgery to save her, but she was too badly hurt. Maria was going to die.

But in the moments right before she died, Maria had something to say. She told the doctors that she forgave Alessandro and that she hoped that he would one day follow Jesus and come to Heaven with her.

The doctors were shocked to hear her words. How *could* she forgive him? And how could she think that his blackened soul might be made clean?

Alessandro was captured and taken to prison.

Then, eight years later, Maria visited him in a dream.

She came dressed in white and handed him a bouquet of lilies. When Alessandro reached out for the lilies, they caught fire. Finally, Alessandro felt the pain of what he had done to Maria and he sank into guilt and sadness.

But he also saw how beautiful her soul was. Suddenly, he wanted to be good. He had tried to drag Maria into the darkness, but she dragged him into the light!

Alessandro remained in prison for many years, but he spent all that time cleaning up his soul. When he was finally released, he became a monk and spent the rest of his days in prayer and sacrifice.

At Saint Maria Goretti's canonization in Rome, Alessandro, the man who killed her, knelt down in the audience, begging for the prayers of the girl who saved him.

Saint Maria Goretti

Born in Italy, 1890
Died in 1902

Maria Goretti was a good and holy young girl, well known for her extraordinary forgiveness of the man who attacked and killed her. That man eventually repented and converted and was present at Maria's canonization. Many people look to Saint Maria Goretti as a model of heroic purity and courage.

VERONICA

Feast Day: July 12

It was a dark and stormy morning—the morning they took our Lord.

As soon as I heard the news, I dropped everything and ran into the city.

I had to see Him. I had to see what I could do to help.

It was madness trying to push my way through the crowds. There were so many angry people. So much yelling and jeering. So many mocking smiles and evil eyes turned round toward me as I found my way forward. *I had to see Him.*

Finally, through an opening in the crowd, I caught a glimpse of His bloody back. All I felt was horror and fear. I wanted to run and hide. I realized that I was too late—*and too small.* There was nothing I could do for our Lord.

But then He turned and looked at me, right into my eyes, as if He were asking for help.

Without thinking, I ran to Him.

Because that's what you have to do when God looks at you. I ran to Him.

Caked dirt and dried blood almost hid His eyes, the most beautiful eyes in the world. If only the whole world could see them!

I took off my veil, leaned close to His face, and wiped away the sweat and the blood there, the dirt and the tears. Why had no one done that yet?

Jesus smiled at me and with those beautiful eyes thanked me for that small gift of kindness.

I wanted to stay close to Him there forever, but the soldiers pushed me away and shoved Him along.

Would I ever see Him again? My eyes filled with tears as I walked away.

Then, when I got home, I found that Jesus had left me a gift—a gift much greater than the one I gave Him.

For when I unwrapped the veil with which I'd wiped His face, it wasn't bloody or even dirty.

On it there was an image of His face. A perfect image of His gentle, loving face. Exactly as I had seen it.

Now the whole world can see it too.

SAINT VERONICA

Died in the First Century A.D.

We do not know much about Saint Veronica's life. What we do know is that she was a kind, generous woman who noticed Jesus as He walked to His Crucifixion. She saw His dirty, bloody face, and she wiped it for Him. Left on her cloth was a miraculous image of Our Lord that has inspired Christians for thousands of years.

Louis and Zélie

Feast Day: July 12

In a little town in France, there lived a young woman and a young man.

One day, the young woman decided to go for a little walk.

The young man decided to go for a little walk too.

In the middle of a little bridge, they met and soon fell in love.

Three months later, Louis and Zélie Martin were married in a big, big church.

But they planned their wedding for midnight, when the rest of the town would be asleep. That way, their wedding could be small and quiet, just like everything else in their lives.

After their wedding, the young couple moved into a small house in which they did small things. Louis was a watchmaker. He worked for hours and hours with tiny gears and screws, making them into something beautiful. Zélie was a lacemaker.

She worked for hours and hours with tiny threads and needles, making them into something beautiful.

Soon, they had little children, and with those little children they did little things. They prayed together. They went for walks. They went fishing, and they admired the flowers.

Zélie made little dresses and hats for her daughters and played dolls with them. Louis played everything with them! He was like a big little child himself.

Not many people noticed the Martin family. They were quiet, and they did small things. But when all those small things got put together, big things started happening.

A hundred years later, Louis and Zélie Martin are now canonized saints. Not only are they in Heaven; miracles have happened on earth because of their prayers.

All of Louis and Zélie's five daughters entered the convent and became holy nuns.

Thérèse, the youngest and smallest, became a Doctor of the Church and one of the most beloved and most powerful saints of all time. Today she is known as Saint Thérèse of Lisieux, but many people call her the Little Flower.

During their lives, not many people knew about Thérèse's parents, the couple who met on the bridge. If anyone did know them, they knew them only as the watchmaker and the lacemaker.

But quietly, secretly, and patiently Saints Louis and Zélie Martin were planting a beautiful garden that will continue to grow through all eternity.

SAINTS LOUIS AND ZÉLIE MARTIN

*Born in France, 1823 (Louis);
1831 (Zélie)
Died in 1894 (Louis); 1877 (Zélie)*

Louis and Zélie Martin are best known as the parents of the great Saint Thérèse of Lisieux. But they were also great saints themselves! Louis, a watchmaker, and Zélie, a lacemaker, loved each other, their children, and their Faith above all else. When Zélie died early of breast cancer, it nearly broke Louis's heart. But their love kept their family strong and holy.

KATERI

Feast Day: July 14

Tekakwitha.

That's what they called her. In her Mohawk language it means "she who bumps into things."

That's because little Tekakwitha couldn't see very well. When she was young, she had gotten very sick and the sickness scarred her face and her eyes.

But even though Tekakwitha couldn't see very well, she knew she would be able to see what she needed to.

One day, Christian missionaries visited Tekakwitha's tribe to teach them about Jesus.

Many people in her tribe didn't want to hear it, for the Mohawk people had always worshipped the spirits of animals and nature and people. In some ways, it was easier for them to worship things that they could touch and see.

But Tekakwitha saw things they couldn't see.

Through the words of the Christian Gospels and the grace of the sacraments, Tekakwitha came to see the love of the One Great Spirit, and it was unlike anything she had ever seen before. She decided to turn away from the Mohawk gods and to follow Jesus.

When Tekakwitha became a Christian, some members of her tribe were so angry, they refused to give her food and even tried to hurt her!

Tekakwitha spoke with one of the priests, who told her about a faraway village where Christian Native Americans could live and worship in peace. Tekakwitha would be safe with them.

So, She Who Bumps into Things left everything behind and walked two hundred miles from New York to Canada. She was weak and couldn't see well, but she found her way.

In the new village, the Christian Native Americans welcomed her and loved her, and there she grew to be very happy and holy.

Instead of Tekakwitha, they called her Kateri, which means "pure," for although her eyes were imperfect, her soul was pure. Kateri was able to see the things that really mattered.

Kateri's health was bad, and she suffered a lot. She lived to be only twenty-four years old.

Miraculously, right after she died, all the scars on her face and on her eyes disappeared. She was smiling.

Finally, she could see the One Great Spirit Himself.

Saint Kateri Tekakwitha

Born in New York, 1656
Died in 1680

Tekakwitha was a Native American of the Mohawk tribe. At eleven years old, she converted to the Catholic Faith and took the Christian name Kateri. Unfortunately, many people in her tribe did not approve of Kateri's Faith, so she had to travel to Canada — a very difficult journey — on foot. There she found the freedom to worship in peace before her early death at twenty-four.

MARY MAGDALENE

Feast Day: July 22

Mary had beautiful hair. She loved to brush it and comb it. She loved to wear it down and long around her shoulders. Most of all, she loved when other people noticed how beautiful it was.

Mary liked it when people complimented her. She liked it when people loved her because of her beauty.

Soon, she grew to like it so much that she liked nothing better. She cared only for the beauty that shone on the outside of her and stopped caring about the beauty on the inside. Her soul became a dark, empty space.

So the devil came and filled it up with horrible fears and feelings and sins.

Mary grew sad. She didn't feel beautiful anymore. Many of the people who had once loved her now hated her because they knew about her dark and dirty soul.

One day, as she was walking through her village, a crowd of people began gathering hard, sharp rocks to throw at her. Mary was afraid they would kill her.

Then, suddenly, a man stepped out of the crowd and sent all the others away. He told them that even though Mary had many sins, they did too.

Besides, He could take away her sins! He could make her soul beautiful again.

And Jesus did just that.

He drove the devil out of Mary's soul and filled her up with His love.

Mary then stopped caring so much about the way she looked. Now she wanted to keep her soul beautiful. And she wanted to give back to the One who had saved it.

So, after that blessed day in the street, Mary went looking for Jesus, to bring a gift to Him. She finally came upon Him having dinner with His disciples. She knelt down before Him, broke open a jar of her most sweet-smelling perfume, poured it over Jesus's feet, and wiped them with her beautiful hair.

Your faith has saved you, Jesus told her as she finished. *Go in peace.*

Mary Magdalene quickly became one of Jesus's most faithful and loving disciples. She stayed close by when He was crucified. She was one of the first to see His empty tomb on Easter morning—empty as her soul once was.

But Jesus was waiting for her right outside it. Ready to make things beautiful again.

SAINT MARY MAGDALENE

Born in Israel
Died in the First Century A.D.

Mary Magdalene was well known for her sinfulness. But Jesus famously forgave her, and she embraced His forgiveness. Mary Magdalene became one of Jesus's most loyal disciples. Despite her sinful past, she was the first to see Jesus on the morning of His Resurrection and the first to believe.

CHRISTOPHER

Feast Day: July 25

Reprobus was the biggest and strongest man in all the land of Canaan, and he wanted to serve the greatest and mightiest king. So he went out to search for him.

First, Reprobus presented himself to the king of his own country. While he was waiting, someone spoke of the devil. Reprobus saw the king cower in fear.

Maybe my king is not that strong, thought Reprobus. *Maybe this devil is stronger.*

So Reprobus set out to find the devil and serve him instead.

Out in the desert, he found a band of robbers who called their evil leader "the devil." *Because this man is stronger than my king,* thought Reprobus, *I shall follow him.*

Reprobus followed that "devil" until the day they came upon a cross and the "devil" suddenly cowered in fear. *Maybe this devil is not so strong after all,* thought Reprobus. *Maybe that cross is stronger.*

So Reprobus set out to learn about the Cross.

Eventually, he found an old hermit who told him about the Cross and about Jesus who died on it and saved the world.

Reprobus, the hermit said, *Jesus is the one to serve. He's the greatest king in all the world.*

But Reprobus didn't know how to serve Jesus.

So the hermit sent him down to the big river and told him to use his great strength to carry people across it—people who were too weak to cross the river themselves.

For years, that's just what Reprobus did.

One day, a little child asked Reprobus to carry him across the river. Reprobus easily lifted the child onto his shoulders and stepped into the river. But with each step, the child grew heavier. Reprobus had never carried anything or anyone so heavy. He became worried they would not make it across the river.

When they finally reached the other side, Reprobus asked the child, *How can you be so heavy? Why did it feel as if I were carrying the whole world?*

The child responded, *Because you WERE carrying the whole world.*

You see, the child was Jesus, and He held the whole world in His hands.

Reprobus soon became known as "Christopher," which means "Christ bearer." Ever since then, strong Saint Christopher has carried Christ to people all over the world.

SAINT CHRISTOPHER

Born in Canaan
Died circa A.D. 251

We do not know very much about the holy martyr Christopher. But this story and the intercession of Saint Christopher have inspired Christians throughout the centuries to be bearers of Christ themselves.

ANNE AND JOACHIM

Feast Day: July 26
(traditional: July 26 and August 16)

It was the best secret I ever kept, that tiny baby girl.

We had been waiting months, years for such happy news. I had nearly given up hope.

But Joachim did not. He told me to keep trusting. God knew better than we did.

There was a reason we didn't have a child yet. And when we did have one, it would be the right one, at the right time.

So it was a cold, bleak midwinter day, and I was feeling down and walking through the fields when suddenly I felt the presence of an angel all around me.

The angel told me a wonderful secret and then told me to go tell my husband.

I'd never run as fast as I did to those golden gates of Jerusalem.

And as I ran, I held my hand over my belly.

111

Baby Mary was too small for me to feel her, but I thought maybe she could feel me. I wanted her to know how happy I was that she was here. I wanted her to know I was the happiest person in the whole world.

When I finally got within sight of the gates, I saw my husband standing there.

Quick in my mind, I thought of many clever, fantastic ways to tell him the great secret. But when he turned to me, I saw in his eyes he already knew. He reached out and drew me close. He kissed me tenderly. Then he put his hand over my belly. He already knew our secret!

Just fourteen years later, my precious little secret had become a beautiful young woman. She was so good and virtuous, better than I was. I sometimes wondered what I had to offer her. She was perfect; I, imperfect.

Then one day, my grown-up Mary told me she had her own secret. She was a little afraid and felt a little alone.

I told her I understood. That I was sorry it had to be so hard. That I was proud of her for being so brave. And then I put my hand over her belly, and I reminded her,

It's the best secret you'll ever keep.

Saints Anne and Joachim

Born in the First Century B.C.
Died in the First Century A.D.

We know very little about Saint Anne and Saint Joachim. But what we do know is that they were the parents of Mary and, therefore, the grandparents of Jesus. Theirs was a holy and happy family.

IGNATIUS

Feast Day: July 31

Everybody liked Ignatius. He was smart and funny. He was a fantastic soldier—quick, brave, and skilled with the sword. He was so handsome that many women wanted to marry him. It almost seemed as if Ignatius was perfect.

But he wasn't.

At least, not on the inside. He cared more about fancy parties, fancy clothes, and fancy swords than he did about his soul.

And then one day, Ignatius's perfect image was ruined.

It happened in a bloody battle with the French. Ignatius's fellow Spanish soldiers wanted to surrender, but brave Ignatius fought on with all his might. Finally, a French cannonball struck his leg and shattered it.

The doctors operated on his leg, but when they finished, Ignatius found that it was not straight. Desperate to look perfect again, Ignatius begged the doctors to rebreak his leg in order to straighten it.

They tried, but they couldn't straighten it.

Ignatius would never look perfect again. For the rest of his life, one of his legs would be shorter than the other, causing him to limp and walk unsteadily. He couldn't be a soldier anymore. Ashamed of his appearance, he stopped going to fancy parties and wearing fancy clothes. Women stopped noticing him. And he lost many of his friends.

But while he lay in his hospital bed, Ignatius had begun to read. He read about Jesus and the saints. He read about their virtues, their deep love, and their great and beautiful souls.

Ignatius already knew how to be brave. Now he wanted to be more than brave.

He wanted to be *holy*. He wanted to *love* more than he wanted to *be loved*.

Years passed, and Ignatius did become holy.

He went to school and became a priest.

Eventually, he founded the Jesuits, his own order of priests. In time, it became the largest order of priests in the world.

By the end of his life, Saint Ignatius of Loyola had many friends again.

These new friends were different from the ones before. These new friends loved Ignatius not because he was handsome and charming.

They loved him because he loved Jesus.

SAINT IGNATIUS OF LOYOLA

*Born in Spain, 1491
Died in 1556*

Saint Ignatius was a soldier and a very popular young man. After receiving a severe injury to his leg in battle, Ignatius became bedridden. During that time, he underwent a conversion. He eventually founded the Society of Jesus, an order of priests devoted to evangelizing and teaching. The Jesuits, as they are called, helped spread Christianity throughout the world.

LAWRENCE

Feast Day: August 10

The good deacon had been coming to visit us for a long time. He would bring us food and clothes and the Holy Eucharist. He would tell us stories, give us blessings, and make us laugh.

He always made us laugh. Even when we were very sick and very sad and very scared. He always found a way to make us laugh.

Then one day, the deacon gathered all of us together and told us he was taking us to the emperor. We couldn't imagine why he would want to take us to that evil man who hated Christians — who killed them!

But Lawrence only smiled, a bit of mischief in his eyes, and said, *The emperor wants me to bring him the treasures of the Church.*

At first, we were confused.

Surely the emperor wanted the money from the collection baskets, not a bunch of us poor, sick people. But Lawrence reminded us that, to Jesus, poor, sick people *are* the treasures of the Church. We smiled ... but what would the emperor think?

Lawrence's eyes twinkled merrily, as he presented us in that great hallway. But the emperor was not merry. He was angry. He was angry that Lawrence had not brought him the money he wanted but even angrier that Lawrence would dare to play such a joke on him.

He was angry that Lawrence was not afraid of him, that Lawrence *really* believed that we *were* treasures, that Lawrence worshipped a King who seemed to give him a powerful kind of courage and confidence.

So he sent Lawrence to the huge grill. To a slow and fiery death.

Surely, this would be the end of his countless jokes.

It's one thing to be brave in the face of death, but to laugh at it? That seemed impossible.

But as Lawrence lay on those hot coals, cooking slowly like a piece of meat, he cracked one final joke.

You can turn me over now. I'm done on this side!

I'm sure the executioners wanted to laugh, but they held their tongues for fear of the emperor. And I think they all knew, as they turned Saint Lawrence over, that they were sending him away to the King of all Treasures and the Lord of Laughter.

SAINT LAWRENCE

Born in Rome, A.D. 225
Died in A.D. 258

Saint Lawrence was a deacon during the time of the Great Persecution. He was well known for his generosity to the poor, his bravery, and his great sense of humor. Because of his strong faith, Emperor Valerian ordered that Lawrence be killed in a frightful way. But Lawrence was not afraid and famously joked with the men who were killing him!

PHILOMENA

Feast Day: August 11

Only about two hundred years after Jesus walked the earth, a young man and a young woman got married. Soon afterward, they became Christians. Then they had a baby. They named her Philomena, which means "daughter of light."

She was born into their new light of faith and brightened their world. They were a very happy and holy family.

Then, when Philomena was just thirteen years old, the cruel pagan Roman emperor Diocletian decided he wanted to marry her.

Philomena refused. She would not give up her Faith.

So the emperor told her about all the riches he had—all the lovely, sparkling things he would give her if she would become his wife.

Philomena still refused, because nothing was more lovely and sparkling than her light of faith.

This made Emperor Diocletian very angry. He put Philomena in prison and tortured her.

For forty days, angels came to Philomena and helped her bear the violence.

The emperor grew angrier. He ordered one final swift attack upon Philomena, an attack that killed her.

She was laid in a tomb in the catacombs—the holy underground tunnels where Christians hid during the persecutions—and quickly the world forgot about this daughter of light.

But not forever! Over a thousand years later, some Christians were digging in the catacombs, looking for hidden treasures, for remnants and reminders of great and holy saints of times past. They came across a small tomb with the name "Philomena" written on it. They didn't know who Philomena was. When they opened the tomb, they found bones and a small bottle with blood in it. When they held that ancient blood of Philomena up to the light, it shimmered and sparkled like rubies.

Quickly, news of the hidden martyr saint spread throughout the world. Christians began to pray for Philomena's intercession, and miracles started to happen.

Then Philomena herself appeared in visions to three people and told them her beautiful story. Devotion to Philomena spread, she was declared a saint, more miracles happened, and they continue to happen today.

That little light, hidden deep in the earth so long ago, is hidden no longer. Saint Philomena shines down from Heaven and brightens the world that tried to destroy her.

Saint Philomena

Born in Greece, A.D. 291
Died in A.D. 304

All we know about Saint Philomena we know from her remains at the place where she was buried and the visions of a nun who was reportedly visited by her. According to the nun's account, Philomena was a Greek princess who became a brave martyr at the age of thirteen. Though her story is mysterious, many people rely on the powerful intercession of Saint Philomena.

CLARE

Feast Day: August 11
(traditional: August 12)

Clare was a beautiful young woman. She wore bright, colorful dresses and precious, sparkling jewels. Many men wanted to marry her. One day, Clare would be a beautiful bride. And she would have a beautiful home of her own.

But Clare had received a special message from Jesus. He did not want her to get married. He wanted her to give away everything she had to the poor and become poor herself! Jesus would be her husband, taking care of her and making sure she had everything she needed.

People thought Clare was crazy when she traded her richly colored dress for one made of brown wool and her shiny, shimmering belt for one made of knotted rope. People thought she was crazy when she cut her pretty, long hair and covered her head with a nun's veil.

You have so many nice things! Why are you giving them all away?

But Clare only smiled: *All I need is Jesus.*

Soon, other women heard the same message from Jesus. They joined Clare, and they all lived together in a convent. They spent their days taking care of the poor and the sick and anyone else who needed help. The Poor Clares didn't have much of anything of their own—not even shoes! But they were still very happy.

How can you be happy when you have so little?

The Poor Clares only smiled: *All we need is Jesus.*

One day, when Clare was older and very sick and weak, an enemy came and tried to attack her convent. The other nuns were afraid. They had no weapons. They had no soldiers. They had no money. They had no way to defend themselves.

But Clare remembered: *All we need is Jesus.*

So she took the monstrance that held the sacred Body of Christ, and she brought it to an open window—a window the soldiers were planning to enter—and she held it up for all to see.

Rays of light shot out from the monstrance and blinded the enemy soldiers. They were terrified and immediately ran away! They wouldn't dare try to hurt the Poor Clares because they saw that the Poor Clares had the greatest, strongest, and most powerful Thing in the world!

And He was all they needed.

Saint Clare of Assisi

Born in Assisi, 1194
Died in 1253

Saint Clare is well known for her friendship with Saint Francis of Assisi. Like Francis, Clare founded a religious order, the Poor Clare nuns, who modeled themselves after the same simplicity as the Franciscans. She is the patron saint of television because when she was sick and unable to attend Mass, she was apparently able to hear and watch the Mass on the wall of her cell.

Maximilian Kolbe

Feast Day: August 14

I didn't want to be a soldier for Hitler. Hitler was evil.

But I was afraid to refuse. They might kill me! And what could be worse than losing my life?

They put me in charge of the starvation cell. It was a horrible job. Horrible watching their bodies die—but even worse watching their hope die. All the light would go out of their eyes.

Then, one day, they sent a new prisoner, Maximilian Kolbe.

He wasn't supposed to be there. The Nazi soldiers had originally selected ten men to send down to the cell, but when one of them cried out for his wife and his son, another man stepped forward.

Take me instead, he said. *I'm a priest.*

The soldiers were confused, but they let the priest take the place of the husband and father.

When I first saw Maximilian Kolbe, there was so much light in his eyes! And I wondered where it came from.

Days passed. We weren't allowed to give the prisoners any food or water. Quickly, they began to weaken. Many of them no longer spoke. Some of them just lay on the ground all day, and it was hard for us to tell whether they were dead or alive.

Except Maximilian Kolbe.

He sat up straight against the cold stone walls. His body was sick and weak, but his eyes were still full of light. Somehow, the weaker he got, the more hopeful he became. He continued to speak. Not only did he speak—he sang! He sang hymns to Jesus and Mary all through the day and all through the night. Some of the other prisoners began to sing with him. I think all of us caught a little bit of his hope.

After two weeks, Maximilian Kolbe was the only prisoner still alive. Since starvation was not killing him, my superiors decided to take his life in another, quicker way. When they approached him, he didn't run or yell or cry or do anything that I would have done. He smiled at the men who were about to murder him, as if they weren't taking anything from him at all!

His eyes shone brilliantly.

I watched his body die.

But I've never seen a man who was so alive.

Saint Maximilian Kolbe

Born in Poland, 1894
Died in 1941

Saint Maximilian Kolbe was a Polish priest well known for his devotion to Mary and his zeal for the Faith. He is best known, however, for the sacrifice of his life, which he offered in place of a fellow prisoner in a Nazi concentration camp and for the great joy with which he endured his final days in a torturous prison cell.

ROSE

Feast Day: August 23
(traditional: August 30)

Isabel was very beautiful. When she was born, her face was as lovely as a flower. So everyone started calling her Rose. But she didn't really like being a rose. She didn't like everyone always staring at her. She didn't like all the women talking about her and all the men wanting to marry her.

She worried that if she was busy watching everyone else's eyes on her, she might turn her own eyes away from God.

So she tried to hide.

She tried to hide from their eyes.

Rose wanted to enter a convent, but her parents would not let her. So she asked them to make a little cell for her in their garden where she could stay and spend her days in quiet prayer.

She cut off her beautiful long hair and wore a veil over her head so nobody could see it. On the inside of a crown of roses her mother gave her, Rose placed little thorns so that the crown would feel more like the one they placed on Jesus and less like the crown of a princess.

But no matter what she did and how much Rose tried to hide, people still noticed her and came to her.

They came for the lovely lace she sewed. They came for the pretty flowers she planted. Even though Rose hid away, they came because they knew her prayers were powerful and could move souls and change people. They came so that she might pray over them and heal them of their diseases and ailments, for she was known for miraculous cures.

Then one day, pirates rushed into Rose's little town of Lima, intending to attack all the Christians. Someone had to stop them!

And Rose knew that she was the one.

She gathered all the people together in the Church and led them in prayer. When the pirates stormed into the church, they saw Rose holding high the monstrance, which was shining in a blaze of glorious light! It shone so brightly that the pirates couldn't look at it. They were scared and ran off.

But the good people inside the church looked up and saw before them beautiful Saint Rose of Lima, the girl who could not hide away.

SAINT ROSE OF LIMA

Born in Peru, 1586
Died in 1617

Saint Rose of Lima was a very beautiful and pious little girl. She liked to be left alone in prayer, and she was known for her extreme acts of penance and sacrifice. Despite her solitary nature, many people sought her out for her help, advice, and prayers. When she died, the people of the city flocked to her funeral to honor her and her holiness.

Monica and Augustine

Feast Days: August 27 (traditional: May 4), Monica;
August 28, Augustine

It was getting late and time for Augustine to go home. He knew his mother would be waiting.

But Augustine didn't want to go home. He felt restless, curious, mischievous. He wondered what it would be like to go the wrong way.

So he and his friends sneaked into a garden and stole fruit from a fruit tree. Lots of fruit, but not because they were hungry. They stole it to throw it away and feed to the pigs. They stole it just for fun.

After that night, Augustine did lots of bad things ... just for fun. And he came home later and later. His mother sat up worrying about him. She prayed and cried until Augustine came home. Then Augustine stopped coming home at all.

Still, Monica waited.

Many people thought she was foolish. Didn't she know what a sinner Augustine was?

But Monica didn't think of his sins. She thought only of the restless nights long ago when she rocked him to sleep. She thought of his first smile, his tiny hands. She thought of the little boy at home. Then she closed her eyes on her tears, and she prayed.

Years passed. Monica grew tired and weary. She began to worry that Augustine's soul was lost forever. Her heart heavy and sad, she sought the advice of the bishop.

To her surprise, he smiled gently at her and said, *A boy of so many tears can never be lost!*

So Monica's heart was strengthened, and she continued to hope for her son.

Finally, Augustine did return home. He repented of all of his sins. Not long afterward, Monica died, but she died with joy in her heart, telling Augustine in her last days that nothing could make her happier than knowing her son was home again!

After his mother's death, Augustine turned their house into a monastery, and he became a priest. Soon, he was a bishop. He cared for the poor and the needy. He preached and taught and wrote many, many books.

His books are like maps — maps that help thousands of others who've turned the wrong way, leading them back home.

SAINTS MONICA AND AUGUSTINE

*Born in Modern-Day Algeria,
A.D. 331 (Monica);
A.D. 354 (Augustine)
Died in A.D. 387 (Monica);
A.D. 430 (Augustine)*

Monica was a holy woman, but her husband was a pagan, and he would not let Monica baptize their son Augustine. For many years, Monica prayed fervently for her husband and children. A year before his death, her husband converted. Eventually, Augustine also turned from his sinful ways and became a brilliant theologian, a holy man, and a saint and Doctor of the Church.

TERESA OF CALCUTTA

Feast Day: September 5

Who IS she? And how does she live with THEM?

People began to wonder at the little nun in the white and blue habit. She used to live in the convent with the other nuns where it was safe and warm and dry.

Wasn't that enough? To pray all day?

Now she lived in the dirtiest streets with the poorest and sickest people in the world. Many of them had horrible diseases, and every time the little nun touched them, she risked getting sick too. People there were dying every day. There were terrible smells. There was sadness in the air. This was a place nobody wanted to be.

So why are you here? They asked her.

But the little nun just smiled. *Jesus made it very clear, she said: Whatever you do for the least of my brethren, you do for me.*

Mother Teresa spent all the rest of her life with people nobody could help very much and people nobody loved — with the least of our brethren.

And then, over time, something remarkable happened. *Everybody* started wanting to spend time with *her*.

Kings, princes, politicians, and movie stars. Priests, bishops, teachers, parents, and children. Everyone wanted to meet Mother Teresa.

But they didn't have to meet her to know her face. Printed in newspapers and books, her beautiful face came to be known and loved by tens of thousands of people. That's because they could see Jesus in her face. They could see His love sparkling in her eyes.

As Mother Teresa grew older — as her skin wrinkled and faded and her body hunched over — as she grew smaller and weaker, we could see Jesus in her even better. Her eyes became more sparkly and her smile sweeter.

Today, there are more than four thousand women who have chosen to live like Saint Teresa of Calcutta, serving the poorest and sickest of the world.

But really, they're serving Jesus.

And He makes them beautiful too.

SAINT TERESA OF CALCUTTA

*Born in North Macedonia, 1910
Died in 1997*

Saint Teresa, or Mother Teresa, as she was called, joined a convent when she was just a teenager. Eventually, she started her own order, the Missionaries of Charity, devoted, like Mother Teresa herself, to caring for the sickest and poorest people in the world.

HILDEGARD

Feast Day: September 17

One thousand years ago, a little girl lived in a little monastery in a little town. She knew very little about the great big world around her.

But inside this little girl's mind, big things were happening. From the time she was just five years old, Hildegard experienced visions. Her visions were like dreams, except she wasn't asleep and she wasn't dreaming. She wasn't sick or sleepy or pretending. In these visions, Hildegard saw things that nobody else could see—things bigger than the whole earth—things bigger than the whole universe!

In fact, Hildegard *saw* the whole universe!

And she saw that the universe was actually quite small, compared with God, who made it.

Hildegard saw the whole universe, shaped like an egg, bursting with life. And inside that egg she saw everything. She saw the earth and the other planets and the sun. She saw the angels and Heaven and Hell. She saw the stars, and she saw the moon.

Hildegard saw everything—the beginning and the end.

But just like a quiet egg in a quiet nest, Hildegard kept all her wisdom hidden away.

She spoke about it only to the woman who took care of her in the monastery, the woman who was like her own mother. Hildegard didn't tell anyone else. She figured no one else would understand.

For years and years, Hildegard watched and listened and waited as, secretly, God filled her up with wisdom.

Then, almost too late, it seemed, when Hildegard was forty-two years old, Jesus spoke to her plainly: *Write down what you've seen and heard!*

So Hildegard began. She wrote and wrote. Books about Heaven and books about Hell; books about the earth and the past and the future and angels and people. She wrote about bodies and minds and souls and the meaning of everything. She painted pictures of her visions and all the things she saw. She wrote music—songs that came from Heaven.

The egg had cracked open, and even today, a thousand years later, we still read and study and listen to the beautiful treasures given to our world by Saint Hildegard of Bingen.

SAINT HILDEGARD

Born in Germany, 1098
Died in 1179

Hildegard was a German nun and mystic. At age five, she began receiving visions from Jesus. When she was much older, she began to share her visions and her wisdom with the world. She wrote many books, composed music, painted works of art, and offered advice on everything from how to be holy to how to bake great cookies.

MATTHEW

Feast Day: September 21

People used to avoid me. When they saw me in the streets, they would turn around and run away. They were afraid that I might call them. And nobody wanted me to call them.

But I never really did have to call them. I would just point my finger and they knew. They knew what I wanted. I wanted their money. And if they had no money, I wanted their animals, their clothes—whatever they could give me.

If they had nothing to give me . . . then they were in trouble.

I didn't really like doing that to people, but I was a tax collector. It was my job. What else was I supposed to do?

Then one day, somebody new passed by my table.

I was all alone, and He was surrounded by people distracting Him. Yet, somehow, He noticed *me* first. He didn't just notice me. He *knew* me. He knew everything about me. And I knew He knew me before He even said anything.

You see, He didn't have to say anything. He didn't have to call me. All He did was point His finger, and I knew what He wanted.

The crazy thing was, this man wanted more from me than I ever asked of anybody! He didn't want my money or my animals. He wanted my *life*. He wanted me to leave everything and follow Him for the rest of my life!

And the even crazier thing was that I was going to give Him what He wanted!

You see, the difference between Jesus and me was that I didn't care about any of those people whom I called and took things from. I used my pointing finger as a weapon. I took without giving back.

But the face behind the finger that pointed at me loved me more than anyone had ever loved me, and the gift I gave to Him would never compare to the gift He gave to me.

In that moment, I stopped being a tax collector.

I became a priest and a writer.

I still pointed my finger at people and called them, but I called them to something wonderful.

I used to bring people bad news. Now I'm a bearer of the greatest news in all the world.

Saint Matthew

Died in the First Century A.D.

Saint Matthew was hated by many because he was a tax collector. But he immediately accepted Jesus's call — "Follow me" — left his old life, and became a fervent disciple. After Jesus's Ascension into Heaven, Matthew went on to write one of the four Gospels, which tell us the stories of Jesus.

Padre Pio

Feast Day: September 23

Francesco loved his Mama very much. She was the one who taught him everything he knew.

She could not read, but she told Francesco many stories about his family on earth and his family in Heaven and how they were always watching over him.

She taught Francesco how to pray so he could stay close to his family in Heaven. She taught him to pray the Rosary, and he held his rosary beads close, as if he were holding his Mama's hand.

When Francesco grew up, he decided to become a priest. He wanted to be good like his Mama and all the holy people in the stories she told him. He wanted to watch over people too.

Francesco became a very holy priest, and people called him Padre Pio. God gave Padre Pio special gifts to help him watch over people in special ways. Padre Pio was able to understand people's thoughts even before they were told to

155

him. He received messages from angels and saints. He worked many miracles, and if he had to help two people at the same time, he could sometimes be in two places at once!

Despite his many gifts, Padre Pio suffered a lot. He was always sick. Enemies rose up against him. The devil tried to hurt his body and confuse his mind.

But Padre Pio never forgot that his family of angels and saints was stronger than the devil, and that they constantly guarded him. Whenever the devil attacked him, Padre Pio closed his eyes, clutched his rosary, and prayed. And the army of Heaven came to his aid.

Padre Pio grew old and very sick, but he never stopped praying. The day he died, though he could barely say the words, he lay in bed praying the Rosary, holding it close as he had once held his Mama's hand.

Suddenly he called out, *I see two Mamas!*

At that instant the people who were gathered around Padre Pio knew that he had crossed into Heaven and was now there with his own Mama, with his Mama Mary, and with all the angels and saints. He was with the family he had loved for so long.

Now, with all of them, he watches over each of us.

Saint Pio of Pietrelcina

Born in Italy, 1887
Died in 1968

Saint Padre Pio was a friar, a priest, and a mystic. He was well known for his miraculous abilities to "read" souls and bilocate. People came from all around the world to confess their sins to Padre Pio. He fought many spiritual battles and endured the mysterious suffering of the stigmata, which meant that he received the bleeding wounds of Jesus on his own body.

MICHAEL

Feast Day: September 29

Long before that slimy little serpent slithered through the paradise of Eden to find and tempt Adam and Eve, he was much bigger and much stronger. At that time, he was not a serpent at all. He was an angel. An angel named Lucifer. Bigger and stronger than all of God's creatures.

But he wasn't bigger and stronger than God.

And he didn't like that he wasn't bigger and stronger than God.

And he also didn't like God telling him what to do.

So he decided to wage war on God.

He convinced other angels to join forces with him and form an army.

It was a strong army, but God's army was stronger.

God placed the angel Michael at the head of His army.

And Michael had something Lucifer did not.

You see, Lucifer relied only on his own power. He was in charge, and he wouldn't listen to anybody. He was filled with pride. So, no matter how big and powerful he may have been, his pride began to shrink him, lower him, weaken him.

But Michael was *humble*. He relied on the power of God. He was ready to listen to his King, listen to His King's commands, and trust in His plans. With God on his side, Michael was by far the most powerful soldier.

And he still is.

The battle between Michael and Lucifer and their armies was fierce, but in time Michael cast Lucifer out of Heaven and down into Hell, where he remains to this day with his rebellious angels.

Usually.

For just as Lucifer prowled about the fruit trees and the peaceful animals of Eden, hoping to lure Adam and Eve into sin, so, even today, he often prowls the earth, seeking the ruin of souls.

But even though Lucifer is still quite strong, Michael is much stronger.

And so, we pray, *Saint Michael the Archangel, defend us in battle. Be our protection against the wickedness and snares of the devil. May God rebuke him, we humbly pray, and do thou, O Prince of the Heavenly Hosts, by the power of God, cast into Hell Satan and all the evil spirits who prowl around the world seeking the ruin of souls. Amen.*

Saint Michael the Archangel

Saint Michael is one of the three archangels mentioned in the Bible. He is the soldier angel—the one who battles against the devil. For thousands of years, Christians have sought the intercession of Saint Michael to protect against all sorts of evils. And Saint Michael comes. And he protects.

GABRIEL

*Feast Day: September 29
(traditional: March 24)*

God made all of the angels strong, but He made Gabriel the strongest: big and great and powerful.

He even gave Gabriel a powerful name: *strength of God!*

But God didn't choose Gabriel to be His warrior.

He didn't choose Gabriel to fight the fierce battle against the fallen angel Lucifer. Gabriel didn't come with leagues of soldier angels by his side. He didn't charge into battle with a fiery sword or a golden shield. He didn't come with trumpet blasts and earthquakes.

Gabriel came gently, quietly, secretly.

Do not be afraid, Mary, he said in secret to a small woman in a little house in a tiny village.

Mary heard him, but no one else did; and she kept his message in her heart.

Do not be afraid, Joseph, he whispered to a humble, kind carpenter in another little house. Joseph was sleeping, but Gabriel came gently, in the quiet of Joseph's dreams.

Do not be afraid, shepherds, he sang down to poor, ragged men and their dirty, poor sheep in a cold and dark field. Usually they listened to no one, but they listened to Gabriel.

Do not be afraid, he told Joseph and Mary, and their newborn baby, as they rushed away with nothing but themselves and their donkey. They were fleeing from the evil king who wanted to destroy them. *They were afraid.* But Gabriel kept them safe.

Do not be afraid, he said softly, years later, as he comforted a sorrowing Jesus, lonely and weeping in the Garden of Gethsemane. That night, only Gabriel, the mighty angel, was strong enough to give strength even to the Son of God.

One day, Gabriel will come again.

Not softly and gently, but with a trumpet blast, loud, frightening, and strong!

That day, fear will overcome the people who have rejected God.

But good souls — gentle souls — Gabriel will sweep up in his strong arms, bearing them swiftly to Heaven by the strength of his mighty wings.

And they will not be afraid!

Saint Gabriel the Archangel

Saint Gabriel is one of the three archangels mentioned in the Bible. He has appeared to many holy people, including Mary, Joseph, Zechariah, and maybe even Jesus in the Garden of Gethsemane. He is the messenger angel, usually bringing tidings of great joy. We also believe that Gabriel is the angel who will come back to earth, announcing the end of the world.

THÉRÈSE

Feast Day: October 1

Thérèse always loved flowers, and flowers were all around her.

Flowers in the garden by her window and flowers in the vase; flowers her mother sewed carefully into lace, and flowers her father planted and watered.

But there were other flowers too.

Like the gentle beauty of her mother's face.

Or the sound of her father's laughter.

There were sunsets and sunrises and little sister giggles.

Love bloomed all around Thérèse.

Then a storm battered the garden. When Thérèse was only four years old, her mother died. Thérèse did not know how she could ever be happy again.

For years, Thérèse's father and sisters tried to cheer her up. Her father took her for daily walks in beautiful gardens and forests that Thérèse had loved so much.

But still she cried—so much that friends told her she would run out of tears!

Thérèse wanted to be happy, and certainly did not want to run out of tears. But then, with her mother already dead, two of her sisters left home to join the convent.

How could Thérèse be happy when the people she loved kept being taken from her?

With a sorrowful heart, Thérèse continued to pray and ask God to help her. One day, ten years after her mother died, Thérèse was going up the stairs after coming home from Midnight Mass.

Suddenly, Thérèse's heart leapt with joy! For right there on that staircase, God told her a secret. He said that trying always to be happy would never make her happy. Instead, she needed to learn to love.

And that's just what she did.

Thérèse gathered up in herself all the love her mother and father and sisters had showered on her. She turned her face to the rest of the world, opened her heart, and let it blossom with love.

Thérèse didn't live a long time. She entered the convent a year after going up the stairs that Christmas and stayed there until she died at just twenty-four years old.

But in her short life, she loved deeply, in all the big and little ways she could.

Today, people call her the Little Flower.

From Heaven, Thérèse showers down love and flowers.

If you ask her, she will shower them down on you too.

THÉRÈSE OF LISIEUX

Born in France, 1873
Died in 1897

Thérèse was a sweet, sensitive little girl born into a loving family. After her mother's death, Thérèse found it difficult to be happy. But she eventually developed her "little way"—striving for holiness in the small challenges of daily life. She entered a convent at fifteen and died at just twenty-four. She is the patron saint of missionaries even though she never left the convent.

FRANCIS

Feast Day: October 4

It started out just like any other Christmas Eve. We had put on our best clothes and ventured out into the frigid midnight air. As we did so, I tried to remember what it must have been like that first Christmas Eve, as the Holy Family rushed through Bethlehem, cold, afraid, and lonely.

But it was always hard to remember. Our Church was warm and filled with light. Midnight Mass was beautiful, but it didn't really feel like the stable in Bethlehem. So it was hard to imagine that very first Christmas. It was hard to remember.

But that Christmas Eve, we did remember. We remembered because of Brother Francis.

We had heard that Brother Francis had something planned. And that's why he had called us out to the little cave. But why? Why would he plan a Mass in a cave?

As we got nearer to the cave, we heard strange sounds—loud sounds! And we smelled strange smells—strong smells!

And then, we finally saw it. We saw the sheep, and we saw the donkey. We saw the cow, and we saw the manger with the hay. Inside that little cave we saw the stable that Brother Francis had brought to our Christmas Eve Mass. We saw, and then *we remembered.*

Brother Francis smiled through the whole Mass. He was transfixed and transported. And I think we all were, a little bit! When the Host was raised above the altar, we all knew it was more than just a Host. But that night, we really felt it. The manger was empty. But only because the altar wasn't. And that night we could really see it. We could really see Jesus.

Brother Francis was the first person to bring the Nativity scene to Mass, but certainly not the last!

Because of his great idea, now nearly every Church in the world has its own Nativity scene on Christmas Eve. You probably even have one in your own house!

On quiet winter nights you might find yourself curled up by the Christmas tree with a donkey in one hand and a sheep in the other.

And just as Saint Francis did, you'll remember.

Saint Francis of Assisi

*Born in Assisi, circa 1181
Died in 1226*

As a young man, Francis was worldly and frivolous, but later he repented and decided to follow Jesus in extreme poverty. Other men joined Francis, and they became known as the Franciscans. Francis also loved animals. There are many stories about him preaching to them and taming them. Saint Francis had a radical love for God's creation that inspires people all over the world.

TERESA OF AVILA

Feast Day: October 15

Little Teresa loved the stories of the saints—especially the stories of the brave martyrs. She wanted to be like those martyrs. She wanted to be like Lucy or Cecilia or George or Christopher. She wanted holiness—and she wanted it *now*.

So, when she was just seven years old, Teresa ran away from home. She'd heard that the Moorish people were persecuting and killing Christians. She thought that if she found these people, they might persecute her too. Then she'd have to be brave. She might even become a martyr! And then, surely, she would find holiness.

But Teresa didn't find holiness.

Her uncle found *her*.

He found Teresa on the road with her brother, and he scolded her for her carelessness. Didn't she know it was a sin to throw away her life? The martyrs were holy because they were brave in the face of death—not because they went looking for it!

Teresa was ashamed. But she was still determined to find holiness.

So she started to pray a little more every day.

When she was older, Teresa, in her prayers, learned about a very special castle—much like the castles in the books she read as a child—a beautiful castle. But this castle was inside Teresa's soul. It was full of many winding passages and wonderful rooms. Some of those rooms were even a little bit scary.

But the more Teresa prayed, the further she wandered into the rooms of the castle. The further she wandered there, the more beautiful everything became and the closer she felt to Jesus.

As she neared the center of the castle, she began to suffer a lot—in her body and in her soul. But she also experienced great joy. Eventually, Jesus began appearing to her and staying with her for a few moments.

In those moments, Teresa was perfectly happy.

Saint Teresa of Avila never did become a martyr. She became a nun, started convents, and taught many people how to pray. Teresa of Avila was never asked to die for Jesus. But she *was* asked to be brave. In her bravery, in the middle of her own winding castle, she found holiness.

Saint Teresa of Avila

Born in Spain, 1515
Died in 1582

Saint Teresa of Avila was a Carmelite nun and mystic. As a child, she loved romances and adventure stories. Her relationship with Jesus became its own adventure—filled with visions and other incredible spiritual experiences. Teresa of Avila wrote several books about prayer and spirituality and is considered a Doctor of the Church.

LOLEK

Feast Day: October 22

Most nights, little Lolek fell asleep easily, lying next to his brother and talking about the day's adventures. But tonight he couldn't sleep. His mind felt loud and the world around him too quiet. He tossed and turned and finally decided to get up.

Slowly, he pulled the covers aside and stepped out of bed. Then he heard something—a shuffling noise on the other side of the room.

Lolek froze.

And then someone spoke out of the darkness.

Lolek, do not be afraid. It's just me.

Lolek's pounding heart slowed. He felt his way through the dark little bedroom, careful not to wake his mother and his brother, until he came to his father's side at the little kneeler.

His father pulled him close, holding him there for a long time. With his father there praying over him, Lolek fell softly back to sleep.

Many years later, Lolek would awaken in the night again.

And again.

He was now the Pope—the shepherd of the whole world!

The troubles of that world weighed upon him. Countries were torn apart by terrible wars. Evil people hated the Pope. Some even tried to kill him! So many hurting people needed his help and his prayers.

Lolek now knew that the world was never really silent. Everything felt loud.

Sometimes, as he lay alone in bed in those great Vatican rooms, he would yearn for the little bedroom he shared with his family and even for his restless, quiet nights there. It wasn't easy taking care of everyone. It wasn't easy being the shepherd of so many sheep.

He loved the world and the people of the world, but sometimes when you love something or somebody so much, your heart gets so full that it hurts.

Lolek felt the pains and the sorrows of his people. He wanted to help them, but it wasn't always easy to know how.

So, on restless nights, Lolek would creep out of bed and tiptoe to the kneeler in his room. It was here that he remembered he was never alone.

Even in the darkness. Even when his heart hurt.

Do not be afraid, his Father would tell him. *I am always with you.*

Saint John Paul II

Born in Poland, 1920
Died in 2005

Born Karol Józef Wojtyła, Pope John Paul II was a man of many talents and gifts. He was a wonderful actor, a skilled athlete, an eloquent writer, and a loyal friend. As a young man, he witnessed the horrors of World War II, but he did not lose his hope or his joy. As pope, he inspired people all over the world with his powerful message: *Do not be afraid!*

ELIZABETH

Feast Day: November 5

It was a warm spring day, the day my cousin Mary came.

I had been longing for a visit from her. I was so lonely, those many months when Zechariah could not speak.

I felt my baby growing inside me. I felt joy and excitement and pain and fear, but I couldn't share it with anybody!

Mary would understand. Mary always understood.

It was a warm spring day, hot even. I hadn't been going outside because I would get tired and dizzy now that the baby was getting bigger. People kept telling me I should sit down, that I shouldn't clean or cook or walk far or run.

But when I heard that cart coming around the bend, my baby started jumping inside me—dancing! He was telling me something! He was telling me to *run*!

And so I ran.

I ran to Mary! I ran with all my might and I wasn't tired or dizzy at all!

Mary's face was shining, her smile warm and bright.

I was much older than Mary, but somehow, in that moment, she seemed older than I was.

Much older!

Tears fell from my eyes as she wrapped her arms around me.

And I was right—Mary did understand.

She understood everything, so much more than I ever knew.

She had a baby in her belly too! All the joy and excitement that I felt, she felt even more. She felt all the wonderful things and all the painful things too. She felt everything I felt, so I didn't feel alone anymore.

I knew that everything was going to be okay. Now, and tomorrow, and at the end of time.

My baby knew it too.

Round and round, John danced inside me ... because he was as happy as I was.

That day, in the middle of that vast field under the shining sun, we met God through Mary.

We touched Him.

We felt Him.

And we *rejoiced*!

SAINT ELIZABETH

*Born in Israel, First Century B.C.
Died in the First Century A.D.*

For many years, Elizabeth could not have children. But when she was very old, she conceived a baby boy who would grow up to be the great prophet John the Baptist. When Elizabeth's cousin, Mary, came to help with the birth of John, Elizabeth quickly knew that Mary carried the Savior in her womb. She cried out with joy the words we all know well: "Blessed is the fruit of your womb!"

MARGARET

Feast Day: November 16
(traditional: June 10)

King Malcolm was the wealthiest man in all of Scotland. He had all the jewels and gold and riches anyone could ever want. But something was missing. He wasn't really happy.

Then one day a storm struck the nearby seas, pushing an English ship onto the Scottish shores. On that ship was a great pearl. A pearl of great price. More precious than anything in King Malcolm's castle.

The pearl, also called Princess Margaret, was very beautiful. But she was even more virtuous than she was beautiful. King Malcolm fell in love with her and made her his queen. He loved his pearl with all his heart and all his soul, and she loved him too.

But Queen Margaret soon taught him about an even greater Pearl of Great Price. She taught him about the Kingdom of Heaven. She taught him virtue. Faith, hope, and love flowed out of the castle. Every day, Queen Margaret welcomed in the sick and the poor, feeding them and washing their feet in the beautiful, bejeweled dining rooms.

The people of Scotland loved their queen, their pearl, and relied on her precious prayers. At midnight, Margaret would wake to pray; in the mornings she would wake to pray; and in the evenings she would stay up late to pray.

Sometimes Malcolm wondered how she ever prayed so much. He didn't understand how she could do it. Didn't she get tired? Weary? Bored? But he loved her all the more because of how much she loved God. And he wanted to find a way to show her that.

So King Malcolm had his wife's prayer books embedded with the finest gold and silver jewels. Now, whenever Margaret prayed, she looked at the beautiful jewels and she prayed even more for her dear husband.

When Queen Margaret was not yet fifty years old, King Malcolm was killed in a battle. Just three days later, Queen Margaret died too. She had already been sick, but sadness and grief made her so much sicker.

But that was okay, because Queen Margaret was ready to be with her husband and their Pearl of Great Price in the Kingdom of Heaven.

SAINT MARGARET OF SCOTLAND

*Born in Hungary, 1045
Died in 1093*

Saint Margaret of Scotland was an English princess born in Hungary who eventually married the King of Scotland. She was well known for her love of the poor and her strong prayer life. She greatly influenced her husband, the king, and all of Scotland to grow in holiness. She is often called the "Pearl of Scotland."

ELIZABETH OF HUNGARY

Feast Day: November 17
(traditional: November 19)

Elizabeth was a strange princess.

She was often seen sneaking out of the castle, her apron full and tied up. The servants and the other royals gossiped and wondered about her.

Where did she go, and what was she doing?

Eventually, the servants discovered that food was missing from the royal table. When they heard that Elizabeth had carried it into town and fed the hungry with it, they were very angry. *That's royal bread she's giving away! Those beggars and thieves don't deserve it. Let the nuns feed them! Our princess and our food should stay in the castle.*

But Princess Elizabeth didn't mind what they said. She kept sneaking out of the castle because she knew she was doing God's work.

One cold winter's day, the king himself was walking toward the village when he ran into Elizabeth. She grew afraid. Although she knew the king loved her very much, she worried he would feel the same way everyone else did. She worried he would be angry with her for taking food from the castle and sharing it with the poor.

The king saw Elizabeth with her apron tied up and full. He asked her to open it and show him what lay inside. Nervously, Elizabeth let the sides of her apron fall.

Much to her surprise (and the king's too), bread did not tumble out. Instead, right there in the middle of winter, dozens of lovely roses fell to the ground.

The king smiled.

Now he understood that the princess was doing God's work and she should not be stopped from doing it.

From that day on, Princess Elizabeth was free to bring bread to the poor and to care for the sick and the needy. At one point, she was feeding nine hundred people every day! She even opened a hospital for them.

Princess Elizabeth lived in a beautiful castle, surrounded by beautiful things.

But she was happy, most of all, because she did God's work.

Saint Elizabeth of Hungary

Born in Hungary, 1207
Died in 1231

Saint Elizabeth of Hungary was a princess who devoted her life to the needy. She provided for the poor, and she started her own hospital and took care of the sick. Elizabeth's husband died early and left Elizabeth very sad. But she did not lose her faith or her commitment to God's people.

CECILIA

Feast Day: November 22

It was Cecilia's wedding day, but Cecilia wasn't happy.

She didn't want to get married.

She wanted to save her heart for Jesus.

She wanted to spend her life singing the prayers of the angels.

But where Cecilia lived, girls didn't get to choose their husbands. Worse, Cecilia was being forced to marry Valerian, a man she didn't love—a man who didn't love Jesus.

Cecilia was stuck.

The wedding ended, and Cecilia went home with Valerian. She was very sad and didn't know how she could ever be happy if she weren't doing what Jesus had planned for her. She didn't know how she could ever be happy if she wasn't singing the prayers of the angels.

But Jesus had promised Cecilia that her guardian angel would protect her, so she didn't lose hope.

One afternoon, Valerian came home from a long time away—a time in which he'd come to know about Jesus and the angels that Cecilia loved so much. He understood Cecilia better now and loved her more. He rushed into their house to find her and to tell her how much he'd changed.

But when he burst into Cecilia's room, he was overwhelmed by the singing of angels. It was the most beautiful music in the world, loud as trumpets and soft as a harp.

It was gentle.

It was strong.

It was mighty.

And it was sweet.

Where it was coming from was not clear as it swirled round and round the room, in the very middle of which stood lovely Cecilia. The bright angel standing by her side placed on her head a glorious crown of flowers.

Valerian became a very good man. He learned to love Cecilia but never forgot that God loved her more. And he let Cecilia live the life of prayer she wanted to live.

Just a few years later, evil Roman soldiers killed both Cecilia and Valerian. Because they were martyrs, they went straight to Heaven.

Today and forever and both together they sing the songs of the angels.

SAINT CECILIA

Born in Italy, A.D. 200
Died in A.D. 230

We do not know very much about the holy martyr Cecilia. But according to legend, she was betrothed to a pagan man despite her desire to remain consecrated to Jesus. However, her holiness inspired her husband, and he eventually became a Christian and was martyred along with Cecilia.

Vietnamese Martyrs

Feast Day: November 24

My eyes felt dazed and heavy. Smoke shrouded everything. I couldn't see or think straight.

When it came my turn and they shoved me toward that fire pit, I closed my eyes. I didn't want to see what they were doing.

At first, the shock of the hot iron on my head overwhelmed me, and for a brief instant, I felt no pain. Then it seared. My eyes shot open, and I screamed.

I looked up at the man who had branded me and saw his eyes. Evil eyes. I fell to the ground and couldn't get up.

But then I felt a gentle hand on mine. One of my Christian brothers had come to help me. When I stood and faced him, I saw it. I saw what was branded on his forehead and what I knew was now branded on mine.

199

Sinister religion, it said in Vietnamese. *Evil*, it meant. *Evil*.

But how could that be? I had seen evil in the eyes of the man who branded it on my face. No, we weren't evil. Evil was afraid of us.

We walked home in silence. Some of the braver ones, some of the more hopeful ones, began reciting the Rosary. I didn't want to keep going. Because I knew this was only the beginning. I knew the persecution would only get worse.

When I got home, I finally saw my face in the mirror. I saw the lie they had burned into it. Tears ran down my face, and I fell to my knees in prayer.

The rest of my days were very hard. But I grew braver, and I grew stronger.

When I looked in the mirror, I no longer saw the lie. I closed my eyes, remembered the Truth, and focused on the One who loved me.

I was eventually killed, along with all my friends.

There were so many of us and the government hated us so much that no one was even allowed to record or to carry on our names. You simply know us as the Vietnamese Martyrs. But there were thousands of us, and God knows all of our names.

Indeed, He etched them in the palm of His hand.

THE VIETNAMESE MARTYRS

Died 1745–1862

It is estimated that up to three hundred thousand men, women, and children were martyred during the various persecutions of Christians in Vietnam. Because of its hatred of Christianity, the government suppressed the records of these saints, so we do not know all of their names. But their stories have inspired Vietnamese Christians and other Christians of all nationalities.

About the Author

When Elizabeth Hanna Pham isn't busy telling stories and raising her four little boys, she likes to play music, go for nature walks, go on dates with her husband, and find creative ways to celebrate the liturgical year.

Sophia Institute

Sophia Institute is a nonprofit institution that seeks to nurture the spiritual, moral, and cultural life of souls and to spread the Gospel of Christ in conformity with the authentic teachings of the Roman Catholic Church.

Sophia Institute Press fulfills this mission by offering translations, reprints, and new publications that afford readers a rich source of the enduring wisdom of mankind.

Sophia Institute also operates the popular online resource CatholicExchange.com. *Catholic Exchange* provides world news from a Catholic perspective as well as daily devotionals and articles that will help readers to grow in holiness and live a life consistent with the teachings of the Church.

In 2013, Sophia Institute launched Sophia Institute for Teachers to renew and rebuild Catholic culture through service to Catholic education. With the goal of nurturing the spiritual, moral, and cultural life of souls, and an abiding respect for the role and work of teachers, we strive to provide materials and programs that are at once enlightening to the mind and ennobling to the heart; faithful and complete, as well as useful and practical.

Sophia Institute gratefully recognizes the Solidarity Association for preserving and encouraging the growth of our apostolate over the course of many years. Without their generous and timely support, this book would not be in your hands.

www.SophiaInstitute.com
www.CatholicExchange.com
www.SophiaInstituteforTeachers.org